IMAGES OF
BODMIN ROAD TO PADSTOW & LAUNCESTON RAILWAYS

IMAGES OF
BODMIN ROAD TO PADSTOW & LAUNCESTON RAILWAYS

CLASSIC PHOTOGRAPHS FROM
THE MAURICE DART RAILWAY COLLECTION

HALSGROVE

First published in Great Britain in 2014

Copyright © Maurice Dart 2014

All rights reserved. No part of this publication may be reproduced,
stored in a retrieval system, or transmitted in any form or by any
means without the prior permission of the copyright holder.

British Library Cataloguing-in-Publication Data
A CIP record for this title is available from the British Library

ISBN 978 0 85704 200 2

HALSGROVE
Halsgrove House,
Ryelands Business Park,
Bagley Road, Wellington, Somerset TA21 9PZ
Tel: 01823 653777   Fax: 01823 216796
email: sales@halsgrove.com

Part of the Halsgrove group of companies
Information on all Halsgrove titles is available at: www.halsgrove.com

Printed in China by Everbest Printing Co Ltd

CONTENTS

Acknowledgements & Reference Sources 6
Introduction 7
1. Bodmin Road GWR/BR to South of Bodmin 10
2. Bodmin General and approaches GWR/BR 19
3. Bodmin SR Branch 32
4. Wenford Bridge Branch 43
5. Boscarne Junction, Ruthern Bridge Branch to Wadebridge East 52
6. Wadebridge 59
7. Wadebridge West to Padstow 82
8. The North Cornwall Line to Launceston 90
9. The Great Western Society at Bodmin 108
10. The Bodmin & Wenford Railway 111
11. The Launceston Steam Railway 149
    Location Index 160

ACKNOWLEDGEMENTS

I express special thanks to my friends, Mike Daly, Terry Nicholls and Harry Cowan for permission to reproduce photos taken by them. Likewise I express thanks for permission to use photos which I have purchased from the collections of the Stephenson Locomotive Society, The Locomotive Club of Great Britain (Ken Nunn collection) and Rail Archive Stephenson (Photomatic). Also my thanks and apologies are proffered to other photographers whose work has been used and not credited. Where no credit is given the photographer is unknown. I also extend my thanks to Steve Jenkins for advice when describing some of the Carriage and Wagon stock. I am also indebted to Simon Butler of Halsgrove for suggesting the idea of this series of books.

REFERENCE SOURCES

A Detailed History of British Railways Standard Steam Locomotives. RCTS.
An Illustrated History of the North Cornwall Railway. David Wroe. Irwell Press
British Railways Locomotive Stock Changes and Withdrawal Dates. 1948–1968. Michael McManus.
GWR, SR, LMSR, LNER and BR Locomotive Allocations for various years. RCTS.
Locomotives of the L. S. W. R. D. L. Bradley. RCTS.
Locomotives of the Southern Railway. D. L. Bradley. RCTS.
My personal notebooks dating from 1945.

INTRODUCTION

At a very early age I was taken to Dockyard Halt, near Devonport and soon afterwards to St Budeaux GWR station to 'watch trains'. I was taught to remember the names of three engines that passed through. At home there was a Hornby Gauge '0' model railway. Most Saturday afternoons my parents would take me with them from St Budeaux to either Devonport, reached by tram, or Plymouth, to which we caught a 'Motor Train' to Millbay. So my interest in railways steadily developed. During the summers of 1937, 1938 and 1939, the three of us spent a week travelling by train to Torquay, Paignton or Goodrington, with sometimes a venture to Kingswear and across to Dartmouth on the 'MEW' or to Dawlish Warren. We used a Family Holiday Runabout ticket for the week and set out from St Budeaux on an excursion train that ran daily from Saltash to Paignton and which, from memory, was usually hauled by a Castle class locomotive to Newton Abbot. From our front windows at Higher St Budeaux I was able to watch trains in the distance as they climbed towards the Devon side of the Royal Albert Bridge. They could also be seen as they rounded the curves west of Saltash station. I asked my father on one occasion why we did not go to Cornwall instead of to Paignton and he replied that it was better to go up the line. This was probably because there was a daily excursion train from Saltash to Paignton although we sometimes had to change trains at Newton Abbot and cross over the footbridge. My father would bring home books about railways. They had been loaned to him for me to look at and they contained many photographs of railway subjects. During the Second World War, following the second batch of blitz raids on Plymouth when many schools were damaged, I was evacuated to Bude by train from Friary. I stood in the corridor for most of the way to "see where I was going" much to the consternation of the WVS ladies who were accompanying us. I recall seeing a tank engine, at what I later learned was Meldon Quarry, carrying 500S on its tank side. This was the T class 'Service loco'. Whilst at Bude I began to hear about places such as Holsworthy and Okehampton, which I had passed through on the train and also Launceston. Evacuation to Bude was followed by a short period back at St Budeaux after which I spent two years at St Austell, using trains to and from North Road. Whilst there, at the evacuated Grammar school, I met many older boys who were railway enthusiasts and my 'railway education' commenced properly.

My father had been transferred from Devonport to the Dockyard at Gibraltar during 1943, and in the summer of 1947 I went there by sea for a holiday for several weeks. My father was an amateur photographer and he taught me to use a box camera. I immediately started taking photographs of Gibraltar Dockyard locomotives from a balcony! On returning to St Budeaux I found my father's two old cameras and managed to obtain a film for each. A large folding Kodak that used A-122 film turned out to have a pin hole in the bellows, only discovered when the results of the first film were seen. This made it unusable. The other was an old Box Brownie which had a push-over lever shutter release and had one good and one faulty viewfinder that showed two images, one above the other. I persevered with this but did not know enough to achieve much success. I tried to record trains passing through St Budeaux and went to Laira shed late in September and took photos, some against the low evening sun. Still, we all had to learn by experience. With those which I had taken at Gibraltar, this was the start of my collection of railway photographs. I saved my pocket money and managed to go on a few Saturday trips to Exeter and as a holiday treat I was allowed to make trips to Bristol and Salisbury. In December 1947 I did a day trip to Gloucester. In January 1948 my mother and I joined my father in Gibraltar which involved sailing from and to Liverpool. We were routed via the North West route to and from Shrewsbury in each direction. In September 1952 I had my first major 'Railway Holiday' and travelled up the North West route visiting loco sheds en route. I visited Liverpool and Manchester and managed to visit some sheds. After a few days at Crewe I returned by the same route to Newport from where I headed to Lydney on Sunday morning to visit the shed, followed by both of the Gloucester sheds and Cheltenham. As time progressed I was able to buy better cameras and commenced longer railway trips to places further afield. My railway interest widened from purely collecting engine names and numbers to encompass signalling and railway history. This was progressed by meeting more very knowledgeable older railway enthusiasts and railwaymen, many of whom became lifelong friends. I developed a desire to obtain photographs of some of the locomotives that I had seen in my early years, so the process of searching for and purchasing photos commenced. As my interest and knowledge grew, so likewise did the quest for more photos. This now encompassed all of Devon and Cornwall and large sections of Wales, along with various classes of locomotives from all over the country. Whilst travelling between Plymouth and St Austell whilst evacuated I had noted the mysterious branch line curving away at Bodmin Road. At that time, one Sunday afternoon I obtained permission to travel by bus to Bodmin alighting outside Bodmin GWR station which was locked up. As return was by the same bus, prowling around the exterior was precluded. Exploration of railways in Cornwall was confined to the main line to Penzance apart from a railtour covering some of the China Clay branch lines in September 1955. Following a work transfer to Cornwall in January 1956 I began to methodically explore the branch lines on spring and summer evenings. I also covered the North Cornwall line several times at weekends. A permanent move to Cornwall during 1988 was followed by visits to the Cornish Steam Locomotive Preservation Society at Bodmin on a few weekends which led to membership. The railway grew and the CSLPS merged with the Bodmin Railway Preservation Society which after several years became the Bodmin & Wenford Railway. Following early retirement at the end of 1990 I joined the B & W Rly on which I became an active volunteer, a position which I still maintain. At times this has enabled me access to some unusual photographic opportunities over the years. Simultaneously I also commenced visits to the Launceston Steam Railway where I was also given some photographic opportunities. An interest in Narrow Gauge and Industrial railways developed. So the 'Archive' steadily grew from filling an expanding suitcase to occupying a considerable expanse of shelf space in two rooms. When it was suggested that I compile some books making use of some of these images I thought that it would be a great idea as many of them, to the best of my knowledge, had not previously been used in publications. Previous books covered Devon, Cornwall, Somerset and Dorset, Wiltshire and Hampshire, Lancashire & Cheshire, and South Wales. Having compiled several volumes around the country I considered it time to return home and compile two local volumes. This is an attempt to follow the routes photographically and to show most of the locomotive types that have worked on them. As historical details of all of the lines have appeared in several publications I have simply compiled detailed captions to the photos. The last two sections contain coverage of the two preserved lines and the photos in each of these are in chronological order. I have attempted to illustrate most of the locos which have operated on both lines but a few are missing. Some older historic images are included but I have attempted to give a good overall coverage of the area to the present day. I have also used some items which are not photographically perfect but merit inclusion because of their content. These images may be of great interest to modellers of historic locomotives with period layouts. I have attempted to make the captions detailed without delving too deeply into railway history or becoming too technical. As this book features images from my personal collection, the layout follows the order in which the collection is arranged. Readers seeking photos at specific locations should refer to the index of locations at the end of the book. Any errors that are discovered are purely attributable to myself. I trust that within the contents there is material to cater for most railway interests and that memories of a bygone age will be recalled.

Maurice Dart
St Austell 2014

1
BODMIN ROAD GWR/BR TO SOUTH OF BODMIN

To save much repetition all of the Beattie Well tanks, the O2 class 0-4-4Ts, the 1366 class 0-6-0PTs and 8750 class 0-6-0PTs 4666 and 4694 were all allocated to Wadebridge shed when photographed. Allocations are given where known for all other locomotives.

This section covers Bodmin Road station and yard and the line to the approaches to Bodmin during the GWR/BR period. At Bodmin Road station I have concentrated mainly on branch line services as so many photos are available of main line trains at this location.

A view of what appears to be a group of GWR Directors carrying out an 'Official Inspection' of the facilities at the newly opened Bodmin Road station in 1887. Maurice Dart Collection/Transport Treasury

Bodmin Road station in the 1930s with wagons in the Goods yards on either side of the main line. The Up side Goods platform is in the right distance as the branch line to Bodmin curves to the right.

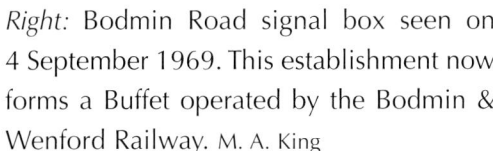

Right: Bodmin Road signal box seen on 4 September 1969. This establishment now forms a Buffet operated by the Bodmin & Wenford Railway. M. A. King

An Up van train approaches Bodmin Road in 1958 hauled by 4-6-0 4931 'HANBURY HALL' from Long Rock shed, Penzance. It is passing the detailed Running In board behind which the Bodmin branch curves right. The Down side Goods shed is on the left. The line which served it was extended as a long siding to serve Bodmin Road china clay kilns. Norman Simmons/Hugh Davies Photographs.

A train from Bodmin General has arrived at Bodmin Road around 5.50pm on 23 May 1961. It is hauled by two St Blazey small Prairie tanks which are 4575 class 5553 and 4500 class 4565. Maurice Dart/Transport Treasury

Around 1946 4500 class 4552 from St Blazey shed waits to depart from Bodmin Road with the normal 2 coach 'B' set on a train to Bodmin. W. A. Camwell

In 1960 St Blazey's 4500 class 4565 waits to depart from Bodmin Road with a train to Bodmin General. W. Reed

In the mid-1950s St Blazey's 4575 class 5521 is at Bodmin Road waiting to depart with a train to Wadebridge. Ken Webber

St Blazey's 4500 class 4565 has taken water and is running round the train at Bodmin Road on 25 July 1958.
B. W. L. Brooksbank/Initial Photographics

St Blazey shed's 4500 class 4574 is running round the Wadebridge train at Bodmin Road at 5.55pm on 15 June 1961.
Maurice Dart/Transport Treasury

The 3.30pm Paddington to Penzance known as 'THE JUBILEE' hauled by Long Rock shed's 4-6-0 5915 'TRENTHAM HALL' enters Bodmin Road as O2 class 0-4-4T 30236 takes water prior to working the 9.50pm to Wadebridge on 26 June 1956. Maurice Dart

8750 class 0-6-0PT 4666 takes water at Bodmin Road before working the 6.17pm to Wadebridge on 21 August 1961.
Maurice Dart/ Transport Treasury

On 16 July 1958 St Blazey's 4575 class 5519 runs around the Wadebridge train at Bodmin Road. Merchant Navy Locomotive Preservation Society Series AS

In June 1955 St Blazey's 4500 class 4559 departs from Bodmin Road with a train to Bodmin General. Ken Webber

The unusual Water Tower with an extension at Bodmin Road in 1956. The extension was required to carry water across the Bodmin branch and loop lines to enable locos to take water while standing at the platform. Roger Holmes/ Hugh Davies Photographs

Bodmin Road station in the early 1960s. An express waits at the Down platform as a DMU for Wadebridge waits to depart at the branch platform. Lens Of Sutton

Laira's 1100hp B-B Diesel Hydraulic D6322 shunts loaded clay wagons in the Up side yard at Bodmin Road on 10 September 1969. Brunel University Transport Collection/Clinker Views

In May 1956 St Blazey's 4575 class 5519 accelerates up the bank with a train from Bodmin Road to Bodmin General. Photomatic (Rail Archive Stephenson)

St Blazey's 4575 class 4585 descends the bank with a train from Bodmin General to Bodmin Road in May 1956. Photomatic (Rail Archive Stephenson)

BODMIN GENERAL AND APPROACHES GWR/BR

The section covers the station, goods yard and locomotive shed together with the approach lines within the Bodmin environs during the GWR/BR period.

In the early 1950s 4500 class 4505 from St Blazey shed approaches the junction of the siding which served an Industrial Estate as it climbs towards Bodmin General with a train from Bodmin Road.
J. Scott-Morgan Collection/R. S. Carpenter

The exterior of Bodmin GWR station decorated for the Royal Cornwall Show in June 1948.

The exterior of Bodmin General station in September 1962. Colin Judge

Station staff and customers laze on the grass bank alongside Bodmin GWR station shortly after it opened in 1887. Steps, now vanished, lead from the platform up to the road which appears to be devoid of houses. The rear end of the Goods shed is on the left. In the centre of the photo is GWR round-ended wagon 22276. Maurice Dart Collection/Transport Treasury

Staff pose alongside a train headed by an 850 class 0-6-0ST at Bodmin GWR in the mid-1900s. At this time the lamp standards were placed along the centre of the platform.

In August 1910 St Blazey shed's 850 class 0-6-0ST 1905 had gone on shed at Bodmin but the regulator had not been completely closed. When sufficient steam had built up the loco moved itself out, ran down the line alongside the platform and mounted the buffers at the end. Luckily no injuries were caused. This loco was withdrawn in October 1936.

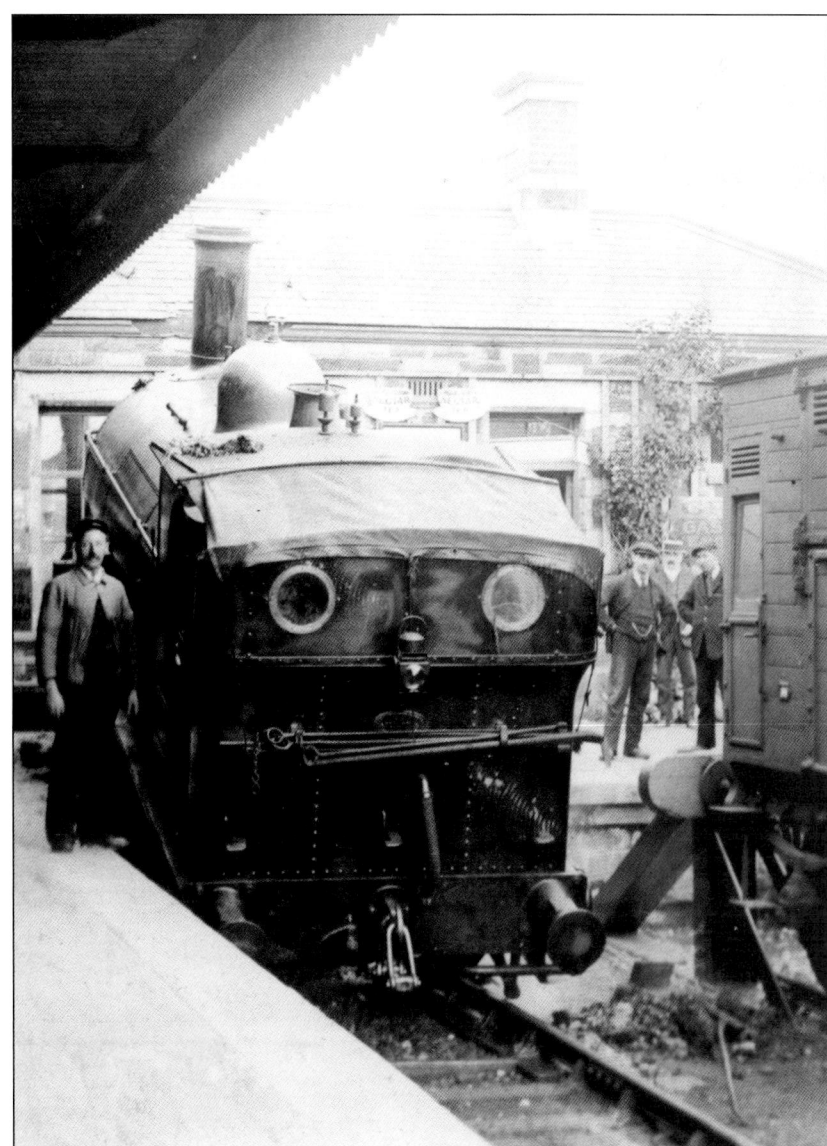

In the late 1930s an assortment of wagons occupy the Goods yard at Bodmin GWR station.

Bodmin General station, Goods shed and signal box in July 1957.

In October 1953 two road vehicles are stabled inside one of several buildings which were immediately south of the Goods shed at Bodmin General. P. J. Garland Collection/R. S. Carpenter

Bodmin General station and signal box and lamp hut in 1952. A small Prairie tank lurks inside the Goods shed. P. J. Garland Collection/R. S. Carpenter

St Blazey's 4500 class 4526 shunts stock at the Goods shed at Bodmin General in September 1956. Harry Cowan

On 9 June 1956 St Blazey's 4500 class 4569 waits with a 'B' set outside the Goods shed at Bodmin General. The nearest carriage which is ex-Works is W6975W. R. S. Carpenter Photos

A scene in the mid-1950s, St Blazey's 4575 class 4585 has arrived with a 'B' set at Bodmin General.

In the early 1950s St Blazey's 4500 class 4526 waits to depart from Bodmin General with a 'B' set.

In 1958 O2 class 0-4-4T 30236 arrives at Bodmin General with train from Wadebridge. Norman Simmons/Hugh Davies Photos

O2 class 0-4-4T 30200 runs around the 6.17pm from Bodmin Road to Wadebridge at Bodmin General on 22 June 1956. Maurice Dart/Transport Treasury

On 13 July 1962 two 1100hp D6300 Diesel Hydraulic locos failed when rostered for duties on the Bodmin branch. As a result Beattie Well 2-4-0WT 30585 worked this Schools Special which has arrived at Bodmin General in a torrential downpour. This was probably the last occasion when a Beattie Well tank worked a Service Passenger train. Charles Whetmath Collection

Laira's B-B 1100hp Diesel Hydraulic D6328 rests at Bodmin General on a weedkilling train on 16 May 1971. Passenger services had ceased and the carriage by the water tower was owned by the Great Western Society who were in residence in the loco shed.

St Blazey's 08 class 350hp Diesel shunter D3526 (later 08411) passes stock owned by the Great Western Society as it departs from Bodmin General for Bodmin Road on 22 August 1971.

Bodmin Lions sponsored a special 'Last Train' on the route to Wadebridge on 17 December 1978. Three car DMU sets B804 and B803 are against the buffers at Bodmin General on the way from Wadebridge to Bodmin Road.

Above: The loco shed, water tower and coal stage at Bodmin General on 25 September 1961. The coal stage is still extant. R. S. Carpenter Photos

Right: In the evening on 5 July 1959 St Blazey's 4500 class 4569 is on shed at Bodmin General. Maurice Dart/Transport Treasury

Below: The interior of the GWR loco shed with the servicing pit at Bodmin General in October 1953. The pit is still extant and is used regularly. P. J. Garland Collection/R. S. Carpenter

Due to a combination of a signalling fault and human error on 7 Dec 1961 the 6.58am Wadebridge to Bodmin General train hauled by 0-6-0PT 4694 collided with a train being shunted by a GWR 4500 class 2-6-2T as it entered General station. This caused a wagon and carriage at the end of the train being shunted to become detached. These two vehicles ran backwards and collided with a D63XX Diesel Hydraulic on a 2 coach 'B' set which was moving over points in front of the signal box to enter the carriage siding alongside the engine shed. The Pannier tank lost its right hand tank and was on Exmouth Junction shed on 31 December in the afternoon. The Hydraulic sustained damage to its front end. The driver on 4694 died of his injuries. The accident was attributed to the train from Wadebridge passing a signal at 'Danger'. The fireman maintained that the signal had been in the 'Off' position but the instruments in the signal box showed it to be 'on'. However problems had occurred frequently in the summer with the wire controlling that signal, it being necessary to increase the tension. With lower overnight temperatures the wire contracted and this may have caused the signal arm to 'droop'. In that position it may well have appeared to be in the 'Off' position to an approaching engine crew.
Cornwall Council/Cornwall Centre

Around 1948/49 O2 class 0-4-4T 203 rounds the curve on the final part of the climb from Boscarne Junction as it approaches Bodmin GWR. Milepost 92½ Picture Library A. W. V Mace Collection/R. S.Carpenter

A lengthy mixed train hauled by St Blazey's 4500 class 4559 tackles the last section of the climb from Boscarne Junction to Bodmin General in June 1955. White on the rim of the front bogie wheel indicates that the loco has recently been shunting in china clay sidings. This was to be seen on numerous locos which were allocated to St Blazey. Ken Webber

3
BODMIN SR BRANCH

The section covers the original and later routes taken by the line from Boscarne Junction to Bodmin SR. A number of not photographically perfect shots are included for historic interest.

In the early 1960s services were revised and new exchange platforms were constructed at Boscarne Junction. On 24 July 1964 W79977 one of the new Railbuses waits on the north side with a service to Bodmin North and a single car DMU waits on the south side with a train to Wadebridge. The small station was officially called Boscarne Exchange Platform but the nameboard carries Boscarne Junction. J. H. Aston

LSWR 0415 class 4-4-2T E050 which was a Wadebridge loco has crossed the bridge over the river east of Boscarne Junction and is approaching Dunmere Junction with a train to Bodmin SR on 8 August 1925. This loco was withdrawn in December 1927. F.H.C. Casbourn courtesy of the Stephenson Locomotive Society

In May 1959 Beattie Well tank 30585 approaches Dunmere Junction with a loaded train from Wenford Bridge. The new route to Bodmin is on the right climbing at 1 in 40. The small shed in the centre which housed the Permanent Way Trolley is on the original alignment which climbed up the bank alongside the Wenford line.
Real Photographs Co. Ltd.

Originally the line to Bodmin climbed, curved and crossed the road a few yards higher up the hill than where the Wenford line crossed. This is Borough Bounds Crossing in 1880 looking towards Dunmere Junction. On the right is Berrycombe Mill with the launder which carried the water visible. A small section of the Water Wheel is bottom right.
Brunel University Transport Collection/Clinker Views

Borough Bounds Crossing in 1880 looking towards Bodmin with Berrycombe Mill and its launder on the left. Brunel University Transport Collection/Clinker Views

Dunmere Halt on the later route to Bodmin in 1934. Brunel University Transport Collection/Clinker Views

Around 1949 O2 class 0-4-4T 30200 climbs away from Dunmere Halt with a short train to Bodmin SR.

Exmouth Junction's N class 2-6-0 31860 climbs away from Dunmere Halt with a train for Bodmin North in May 1962. Wadebridge shed would use any available permitted loco to work these services. Ken Webber

Looking along the line to Bodmin North from the first overline bridge west of the station in January 1964. The signal box is in the distance partly hidden by the nearest signal. Frank Sperritt

A closer view of the signal box at Bodmin North in January 1964. Frank Sperritt

It has been stated by some people that 1366 class 0-6-0PT locos did not work to Bodmin North. To firmly disprove that statement 1369 pauses near the gasometers on the approach to Bodmin North on 24 July 1964. The leading wagon is Shell BP tank 6551. J. H. Aston

LSWR Directors on an Inspection Special hauled by 0-4-0ST 'BODMIN' which is stopped alongside the sand drops at Bodmin Town Old Wharf in 1886. Sea sand for use as a fertiliser can be seen below the sand drops.

Wagons await unloading at Bodmin Wharf around 1890. The bay windows on the right fronted an upstairs waiting room for intending passengers. The legendary Sam Worth is in the right distance standing by a wagon.
Brunel University Transport Collection/Clinker Views

The first Beattie Well tank at Wadebridge was 248 which arrived in June 1893 and departed to Nine Elms in May 1895. This loco was withdrawn in December 1898. Wharfinger Sam Worth poses with staff in front of this loco at Bodmin Wharf. Sam Worth joined the Bodmin & Wadebridge Railway when it opened in 1834. Bodmin Town Museum

Staff pose alongside Wadebridge allocated LSWR Steam Railmotor No.8 at Bodmin probably soon after its arrival in 1906. These worked the service from 1906 until 1914. This Railmotor was withdrawn in November 1916. The locomotive section was scrapped in 1921 and the carriage section was converted into a trailer car. Bodmin & Wenford Railway

During torrential rain (in 1936?) the Town Leat which ran behind buildings on the left overflowed its banks and poured through Bodmin SR station into the yard. Bodmin Town Museum

O2 class 0-4-4T 30192 waits to depart from Bodmin North with a mixed train on 22 May 1952. The coaching stock is Set No. 25. R. K. Blencowe Collection

O2 class 0-4-4T 203 has uncoupled from the train at Bodmin SR and waits to run round in 1939. A. G. Ellis

In September 1958 O2 class 0-4-4T 30236 waits to depart from Bodmin North with a Wadebridge train which is Set No. 29. Harry Cowan

Exmouth Junction shed's West Country class 4-6-2 21C116 (later 34016) undergoing its naming ceremony at Bodmin SR on 28 August 1946 in pouring rain.

8750 class 0-6-0PT 4694 prepares to run round Set No. 24 at Bodmin North in 1963.

Ivatt 2P 2-6-2T 41295 from Wadebridge shed waits to depart from Bodmin North on a wet day early in 1964. Frank Sperritt

Diesel Railbus W79977 waits to depart from Bodmin North for Boscarne Junction on 24 July 1964. J. H. Aston

4
WENFORD BRIDGE BRANCH

This section covers the line from Boscarne Junction to Wenford Bridge and part of the extension to De Lank Quarry. In early days the route to Wenford Bridge was regarded as the Main line and the routes to Bodmin and Ruthern Bridge as Branch lines.

After shunting at Boscarne Junction 1366 class 0-6-0PT 1369 sets off with empty wagons for Wenford on 19 April 1963. P. H. Groom

The same loco, 1369 takes the Wenford branch at Dunmere Junction with a short train of empties in September 1962. Ken Webber

Beattie Well tank 30585 takes water at the well known watering point at Penhargard on 19 June 1958 en-route to Wenford. C. Gammell

Beattie Well tank 30587 pauses on the way to Wenford to shunt at Tresarrett Wharf in June 1960. Harry Cowan

Shortly after 1876 0-4-0ST 'BODMIN' is collecting loaded clay wagons from the siding south of Tresarrett level crossing. The wagons are under the 'FP' shed which was called 'The Patent System'. FP were the initials of manager Frank Parkyn who is standing on the frame of the loco. A modern coal fired pan kiln was erected on this site, known as Stump Oak.

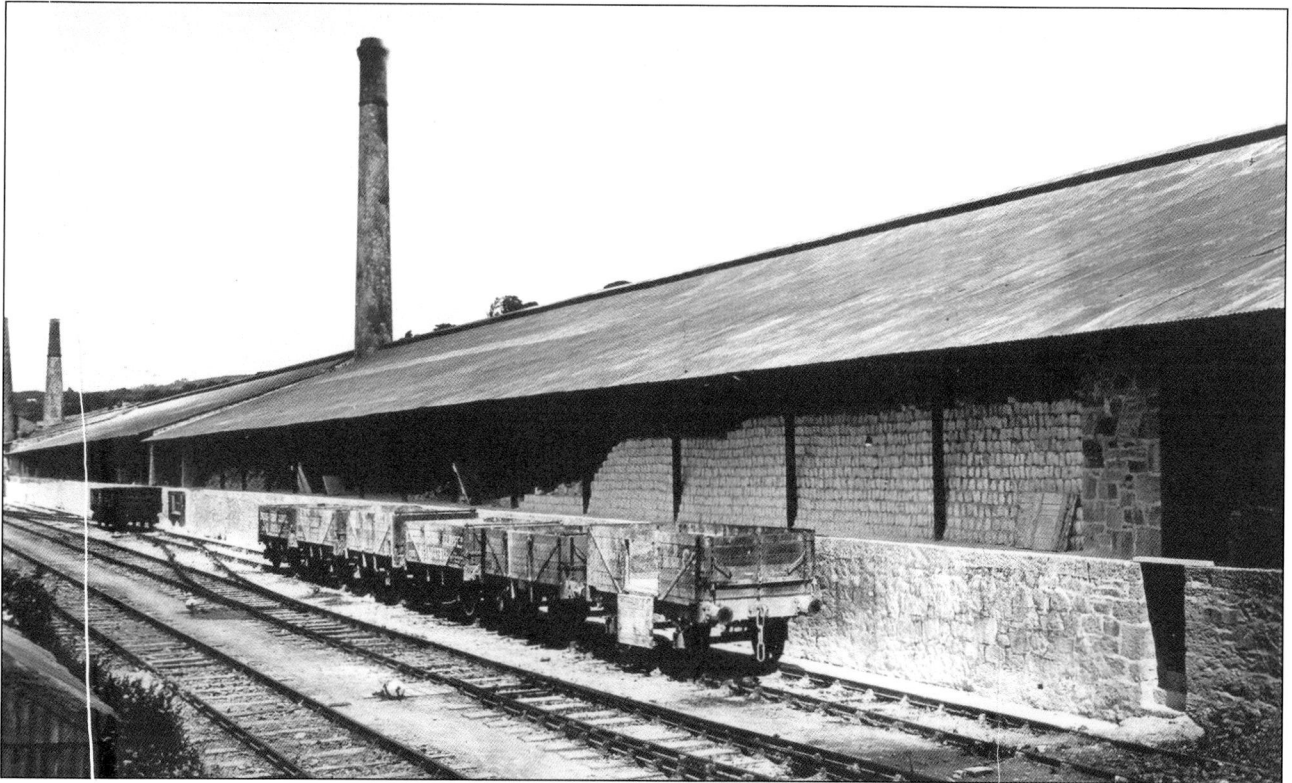

Sidings alongside Wenford Nos. 4 and 5 kilns in the 1930s. There was a line of six pan kilns here. China Clay History Society

Sidings at Wenford No. 6 which the most southerly kiln in the 1930s. On the left by the linhay is GWR End Tip clay wagon 94051 which bears the legend 'Return loaded to Fowey'. China Clay History Society

Beattie Well tank 30587 shunts at Wenford kilns in July 1960. Bagged clay was loaded into the covered vans. Due to the constricted space available the cabside numerals on this loco were of the style used for diesel locos. This was the only one of the trio so treated. Hugh Davies Photographs

A loaded train hauled by St Blazey's 350hp 0-6-0 Diesel shunter D4013 (later 08845) waits to depart from Wenford on 9 September 1969. It is alongside Nos. 1 and 2 kilns. Brunel University Transport Collection/Clinker Views

Beattie Well tank 30586 rounds the curve as it approaches Wenford Bridge in August 1948. Modifications to the watering point at Penhargard in 1952 lowered the filler hose. As the tank filler cap on this loco was placed higher than on the other two locos, 30586 was only used if the others were unavailable for duty. Locomotive & General Railway Photographs

In 1910 a Beattie Well tank prepares to leave Wenford Bridge with a train loaded with granite from De Lank Quarry. The granite blocks were destined for Hartlepool. On the right at the rear of the train is LSWR 'Road Van' 6986. These large brake vans were fitted with doors on their sides to facilitate collection and delivery of parcels.
Brunel University Transport Collection/Clinker Views

Beattie Well tank 30585 and two staff are engaged in shunting operations at Wenford Bridge in May 1959.
Real Photographs

In the late 1920s Beattie Well tank E0314 (later 30585) waits to depart from Wenford Bridge. The loco still carries its Adams stovepipe chimney.

The very last train at Wenford Bridge as St Blazey's 350hp 0-6-0 Diesel shunter D4009 (became 08841) arrives with a brake van from Boscarne Junction in June 1971. The line north of Wenford China Clay sidings had closed to Goods traffic on 13 February 1967. Smoke from Wenford kilns can be seen in the distance to the right of centre. Ken Webber

In the late 1930s Beattie Well tank 3298 (later 30587) rests at Wenford Bridge between shunting. C. Powell

The end of the sidings at Wenford Bridge on 6 July 1949. The private line to De Lank Quarry crossed the road and passed through the gate to reach the foot of the incline to Lower Lank. J. H. Aston

Looking down the incline from the bridge at Lower Lank on 9 June 1934.
Brunel University Transport Collection/Clinker Views

On 6 July 1949 rails lead up the overgrown incline to Lower Lank.
J. H. Aston

Charles Clinker stands alongside the track at the top of the incline by the bridge over a minor road at Lower Lank in the 1930s. The line continued for roughly two-thirds of a mile to the quarry.

5

BOSCARNE JUNCTION TO WADEBRIDGE EAST AND THE RUTHERN BRIDGE BRANCH

This section covers the later route and part of the old alignment from Boscarne Junction to near the site of Wadebridge Junction. The Ruthern Bridge branch is included.

In the mid-1950s St Blazey's 4500 class 2-6-2T 4569 passes Boscarne Junction with a service to Wadebridge. Hugh Davies Photographs

During Whitsun 1982 Laira's 1100hp B-B Diesel Hydraulic D6338 passes Boscarne Junction with a train to Wadebridge. On the right is part of BR Standard 16T Mineral wagon B169460. Roger Holmes/Hugh Davies Photographs

Two of the LSWR special wagons for carrying china clay in containers, from Wenford to Padstow at Boscarne Junction around 1920. The nearest wagon is 4133 and they are lettered N C C C C L which stands for the North Cornwall China Clay Company Limited. It is suspected that these wagons had been specially repainted for some publicity photos.

In August 1959 O2 class 0-4-4T 30200 passes Boscarne Junction signal box with a train to Bodmin North.
R. K. Blencowe Collection

In 1960 8750 class 0-6-0PT 4694 passes Boscarne Junction on a service to Bodmin North.

An unusual view taken from the footplate of a 4575 class 2-6-2T approaching Boscarne Junction with a train to Bodmin Road in the mid-1950s. The photographer was a signalman at Wadebridge. Ken Webber

An unusually busy scene at Nanstallon Halt in the early 1950s.

Custom at Grogley Halt in the early 1950s. The trackbed of the branch line to Ruthern Bridge is on the right crossing the bridge over the River Camel. The branch was accessed by a back shunt on to a siding which ran behind the platform on part of the original alignment.

Grogley Halt in the late 1950s after the original platform had been replaced by an Exmouth Junction concrete structure.

On 29 June 1888 a party of LSWR Directors carry out an inspection of the re-aligned route at Grogley Halt using Bodmin & Wadebridge Railway stock. The track in the bottom left corner is on the original alignment. Locomotive & General Railway Photographs

A view from the river bank on 21 July 1993 of the bridge which carried the Ruthern Bridge branch across the River Camel. Maurice Dart

The Ruthern Bridge branch passed over three minor roads by ungated crossings. This is the first crossing east of the terminus where the line crossed the road to Burlawn on 11 June 1934. Brunel University Transport Collection/Clinker Views

The loop west of Ruthern Bridge terminus in 1930. Brunel University Transport Collection/Clinker Views

In the 1920s a solitary wagon stands near the points at Ruthern Bridge terminus. Behind the photographer the route split into two lines, one of which passed over coal drops. Cornwall Council/Cornwall Centre

Ruthern Bridge Depot with Wharfinger 'Granny Inch' standing in the doorway possibly around 1920. The Depot at Ruthern Bridge served local mines and later served as a railhead for agricultural produce. The term 'Wharfinger' was peculiar in railway terminology to the Bodmin & Wadebridge Railway and is believed to have been derived from the canal era. Granny Inch was the only female Wharfinger. This structure which was on the opposite side of the road to the railway was demolished some years after the branch line closed. Bodmin Town Museum

The 9.48am from Wadebridge to Bodmin North hauled by O2 class 0-4-4T 30203 is near the site of Wadebridge Junction on 17 September 1953. The physical junction was removed and the signal box was closed in July 1907, the routes thereafter being two parallel single lines. T. G. Wassel/Hugh Davies Photographs

6
WADEBRIDGE

This section provides extensive coverage of the station, Goods yard, locomotive shed and quay with a few of the approaches. As so many photos are included this section is arranged by locomotive types. Several photos of Beattie Well tanks and T9 class 4-4-0s are included as these types are so popular.

Exmouth Junction's T9 class 4-4-0 30711 has passed the site of Wadebridge Junction as it approaches the station on a North Cornwall line train on 10 July 1952.

Seen in mid-1962 Laira's 1100hp B-B Diesel Hydraulic D6341 approaches Wadebridge with a train from Bodmin Road.
Mike Daly

Around August 1925 Wadebridge's 0415 class 4-4-2T E050 passes Guineaport with a one coach train for Bodmin SR. F.H.C. Casbourn courtesy of the Stephenson Locomotive Society

St Blazey's 2021 class 0-6-0PT 2127 which is fitted with a domeless boiler passes Guineaport with the 9.47am from Wadebridge to Bodmin Road in March 1926. F.H.C. Casbourn courtesy of the Stephenson Locomotive Society

On 19 August 1958 Exmouth Junction's Battle Of Britain class 4-6-2 34081 '92 SQUADRON' approaches Wadebridge station with the Down Atlantic Coast Express. Wadebridge East signal box is behind the train. A.E. Bennett

Two Exmouth Junction locos double head a North Cornwall line service at Wadebridge on 5 July 1952. The train is hauled by T9 class 4-4-0 30711 which is piloted by N class 2-6-0 31844. Beattie Well tank 30587 peeps out beside the N class. The Goods shed is on the left. T. C. Cole

An atmospheric shot of Exmouth Junction's N class 2-6-0 31406 alongside the coal stage at Wadebridge shed on 27 April 1963.
Maurice Dart

Exmouth Junction's N class 2-6-0 31841 stands outside the back of Wadebridge shed on 5 June 1957. 'Chippendale' has been daubed on its tender.
Maurice Dart/Transport Treasury

U class 2-6-0 31804 from Exmouth Junction stands outside the back of Wadebridge shed on 24 July 1956. This loco was allocated to the Exeter shed for around seven months. *Maurice Dart/Transport Treasury*

0415 class 4-4-2T E050 is at home on Station Pilot duty at Wadebridge around 1925.

Here 0415 class 4-4-2T E050 is stopped by the water column at home at Wadebridge shed around 1925.
F.H.C. Casbourn courtesy of the Stephenson Locomotive Society

Exmouth Junction's T9 class 4-4-0 721 enters Wadebridge with a North Cornwall line train in the mid-1930s.

On 9 August 1948 Exmouth Junction's T9 class 4-4-0 725 waits to depart from Wadebridge with a North Cornwall line train. R. Cogger

Still carrying a 70F Fratton shedplate T9 class 4-4-0 30726 which had been transferred to Exmouth Junction two weeks earlier takes water at Wadebridge shed on 21 June 1958. This was a 'new' loco for me and I had not expected to 'cop' a loco at Wadebridge shed! Maurice Dart

O2 class 0-4-4T 181 fitted with a Drummond boiler is on shed at Wadebridge on 5 July 1948. This loco was transferred to the Isle of Wight in April 1949 where it was renumbered W35 and named 'FRESHWATER'.
J. H. Aston

O2 class 0-4-4T E182 on Station Pilot duty at Wadebridge on 6 August 1928. Locomotive Club Of Great Britain/Ken Nunn Collection

Around 1949 O2 class 0-4-4T 30193 is under repair at Wadebridge shed.

O2 class 0-4-4T E198 stands outside the back of Wadebridge shed on 21 September 1936. In April 1949 this loco was transferred to the Isle Of Wight where it was renumbered W36 and named 'CARISBROOKE'. Arthur J. G. Jarvis/Midland Railway Trust

Rather grubby O2 class 0-4-4T 216 acts as Station Pilot at Wadebridge on 25 July 1933. A. G. Ellis

Retaining a stovepipe chimney Beattie Well tank 0298 loiters at Wadebridge on 6 August 1928. Locomotive Club Of Great Britain/Ken Nunn Collection

In the 1930s Beattie Well tank 3298 approaches the water column at Wadebridge shed. An N class 2-6-0 is in the background. Rail Archive Stephenson (Photomatic)

This photo which is dated 12 October 1921 shows a Beattie Well tank on Station Pilot duty at Wadebridge numbered 314. According to official records this loco was placed on the Duplicate List and renumbered 0314 in May 1901. P. J. T. Reed

In May 1925 Beattie Well tank 0314 sits on the turntable at Wadebridge shed. Real Photographs Co. Ltd.

Beattie Well tank 329 is stopped near Guineaport on a train. As this loco was placed on the Duplicate List and renumbered 0329 in November 1901. This photo probably just pre-dates that.

Retaining its s tovepipe chimney Beattie Well tank E0329 is at Wadebridge shed in the late 1920s. Rail Archive Stephenson (Photomatic)

Beattie Well tank 3329 shunts the Goods shed at Wadebridge in 1947. C.M. & J. M. Bentley

S11 class 4-4-0 400 outside the back of Wadebridge shed on 10 August 1922. S11s 398 and 399 were allocated to Wadebridge for North Cornwall line duties around 1921.

In the early 1920s A12 class 'Jubilee' 0-4-2 533 takes water at Wadebridge shed. This loco was withdrawn in October 1929. A. G. Ellis

A12 class 'Jubilee' 0-4-2 E643 on shed at Wadebridge on 6 August 1928. This loco worked until July 1947.
Locomotive Club Of Great Britain/Ken Nunn Collection

Exmouth Junction's X6 class 4-4-0 E662 outside Wadebridge station on 6 August 1928. Withdrawal took place in March 1933. Locomotive Club Of Great Britain/Ken Nunn Collection

Carrying its SBZ shed stencil and an unusually highly placed buffer beam number St Blazey's 4500 class 2-6-2T 4503 waits to depart from Wadebridge with a train to Bodmin Road on 7 July 1949. H. C. Casserley

In the mid-1950s St Blazey's 4575 class 2-6-2T 5502 waits at Wadebridge with a train to Bodmin Road.

St Blazey's 4575 class 2-6-2T 5570 waits at Wadebridge with a service to Bodmin Road in mid-1960. Ken Webber

Still carrying an 87C Danygraig shedplate newly arrived 8750 class 0-6-0PT 4666 waits to depart from Wadebridge on 1 January 1960 with a train to Bodmin North. Maurice Dart/Transport Treasury

Inside Wadebridge shed on 1 January 1960 are newly arrived 8750 class 0-6-0PT 4694 and old faithful O2 class 0-4-4T 30200. Maurice Dart/Transport Treasury

On 27 April 1963 1366 class 0-6-0PT 1367 performs Station Pilot duty at Wadebridge. Maurice Dart

1366 class 0-6-0PT 1368 is Station Pilot at Wadebridge on 12 March 1964. R. K. Blencowe Collection

Wadebridge's Ivatt 2MT 2-6-2T 41295 passes Wadebridge East signal box from where the photo was taken on a service from Bodmin North formed by SR Maunsell Set 199 late in 1963. Ken Webber

Exmouth Junction's Standard 3MT 2-6-2T 82042 enters Wadebridge station with a North Cornwall line service on 2 January 1965.

Exmouth Junction's Standard 4MT 2-6-4T 80039 moves past Wadebridge shed in 1964. These locos worked North Cornwall line trains for a period and one was usually sub-shedded at Okehampton. Rex Conway Collection

In 1964 Exmouth Junction's Standard 4MT 2-6-4T 80064 rests outside the back of Wadebridge shed. Rex Conway Collection

During the Second World War an Armoured train was stationed at Wadebridge between July 1940 and August 1941. It commenced operating in November 1940 patrolling lines in the area. The trains were identified by letters and armoured train D is at Wadebridge. The loco is LNER F4 class 2-4-2T 7178. Visible around the shed in the background are two O2 class 0-4-4Ts and a T9 class 4-4-0. North Woolwich Station Museum Collection/Transport Treasury

The last Passenger train on the line was organised by Bodmin Lions. At Wadebridge on 17 December 1978 are DMU three-car sets B804 and B803.

Around July 1964 one of the new Railbuses, W79977, stands at Wadebridge. This Railbus operated the service between Bodmin North and Boscarne Junction. *Ken Webber*

In the early 1950s the second building on the left is the original Bodmin & Wadebridge Railway locomotive shed. A low building separates it from the original carriage shed. These structures were demolished during 1962. *T. J. Edgington*

Wagons stand in the sidings at Wadebridge Quay in the mid-1950s. Mike Daly

Beattie Well tank 30586 runs along the shoreline in June 1962 as it approaches Wadebridge with the school train from Padstow. Ken Webber

7
WADEBRIDGE WEST TO PADSTOW

Covering the line from west of the environs of Wadebridge to Padstow.

Laira's O3 class 204hp 0-6-0D shunter D2177 is working a track-lifting train west of Wadebridge on 1 March 1968. Cornwall Council/ Cornwall Centre

Around 1960 Exmouth Junction's T9 class 4-4-0 30338 skirts the river after departing from Padstow with a North Cornwall line train. Ken Webber

An O2 class 0-4-4T has crossed the bridge over Little Petherick creek with a train to Bodmin SR in the early 1930s. Rail Archive Stephenson (Photomatic)

Exmouth Junction's West Country class 4-6-2 34038 'LYNTON' on the turntable at Padstow in 1960. Hugh Davies Photographs

On 4 July 1963 Exmouth Junction's N class 2-6-0 31839 waits to depart from Padstow on a North Cornwall line service. R. K. Blencowe Collection

Exmouth Junction's T9 class 4-4-0 30708 runs around Maunsell Set No. 28 at Padstow on 26 June 1956. Maurice Dart

On 5 July 1952 Exmouth Junction's T9 class 4-4-0 30711 waits on a train for the North Cornwall line in the carriage sidings at Padstow.

In 1948 O2 class 0-4-4T 200 is at Padstow at the head of a train to Bodmin SR. On the right are SR carriages 1284 and 1285. Milepost 92½ Picture Library, A. W. V. Mace Collection/ R. S. Carpenter

St Blazey's 4575 class 2-6-2T 5502 waits to depart from Padstow with a train to Bodmin Road on 7 June 1949. R. J. Buckley/Initial Photographics

In 1963 Wadebridge's Ivatt 2MT 2-6-2T 41275 waits to run around the train at Padstow.

Around 1964 Exmouth Junction's Standard 4MT 2-6-4T 80064 waits on coaching stock at Padstow. Ken Webber

Sometime between 1915 and 1918 LSWR Steam Railmotor No. 10 waits to depart from Padstow with a service to Bodmin. Locomotive & General Railway Photographs

Four of the special wagons for carrying china clay owned by the North Cornwall China Clay Company are at the end of a siding on Padstow Quay around 1920. These wagons have probably been specially repainted for publicity purposes. China Clay History Society

A long line of assorted wagons and vans stand on one of the sidings on Padstow Quay in the late 1930s. Aero Pictorial Ltd.

A variety of rolling stock is present at Padstow in 1905. Bottom right is LSWR round-ended tarpaulin bar wagon 10208. The covered van next to it is 12342. Cornwall County Council/Cornwall Centre.

8
THE NORTH CORNWALL LINE TO LAUNCESTON

This includes the route from Wadebridge Junction to Launceston which town receives good coverage of the SR system, together with intermediate stations and a couple of shots of the siding which served Delabole slate quarry. Launceston GWR is not included as it was not part of this route.

In the late 1900s 380 class 'Steamroller' 4-4-0 383 (?) from Exmouth Junction runs tender first with what appears to be an Engineer's train across the bridge over the River Camel near Wadebridge Junction. This loco was withdrawn in December 1913.

In the late 1950s Exmouth Junction's Battle Of Britain class 4-6-2 34061 '73 Squadron' departs from St Kew Highway with a Padstow train formed from BR Standard Set 567. David Lawrence/Hugh Davies Photos

On 27 April 1963 restored T9 class 4-4-0 120 which was based at Eastleigh heads Plymouth Railway Circle's 'North Cornishman' Railtour as it stopped at St Kew Highway to permit an Up working to pass. Maurice Dart/Transport Treasury

The Up platform and station buildings at St Kew Highway in the early 1950s. C. Powell

The north-east portal of 354yd Trelill tunnel seen from the footplate of an N class 2-6-0 in the mid-1950s. This tunnel is reputed to be haunted. Mike Daly

The Up platform, signal box and station building at Port Isaac Road in the early 1950s. Lens Of Sutton

Exmouth Junction's N class 2-6-0 31812 stopped at Delabole on an Up working in Spring 1964. David Lawrence/Hugh Davies Photos

A three-car DMU for Padstow departs from Delabole in 1965. David Stacey

A horse-drawn conveyance carrying guests, who are well wrapped up against the prevailing weather, to Delabole station. They pass alongside the siding from the slate quarry following a visit in the early 1920s. Piles of stacked slates are in the background.

This obviously posed photograph shows a train being loaded with slate at Delabole quarry around 1912. The train is hauled by A12 class 'Jubilee' 0-4-2 631 which would have been allocated to Exmouth Junction. Nearest to the loco is LSWR round-ended tarpaulin bar wagon 472. Royal Institution Of Cornwall/Royal Cornwall Museum.

Exmouth Junction's N class 2-6-0 31834 enters Camelford on an Up parcels working in the late 1950s. David Lawrence/Hugh Davies Photos

The Down platform and goods yard at Camelford in the early 1950s. The station nameboard invites passengers to change for Boscastle and Tintagel. Lens Of Sutton

An Up goods hauled by Exmouth Junction's N class 2-6-0 31849 enters Otterham in the mid-1950s. David Lawrence/Hugh Davies Photos

Plymouth Railway Circle's 'North Cornishman' Railtour headed by restored T9 class 4-4-0 120 is stopped at Otterham on its way to Wadebridge on 27 April 1963. Maurice Dart/Transport Treasury

Tresmeer station looking towards Launceston in the late 1950s. David Lawrence/Hugh Davies Photos

A track-lifting train hauled by St Blazey's class O3 204hp 0-6-0 Diesel shunter D2127 is at Tresmeer early in 1967. Transport Treasury

The Up platform, station buildings and signal box at Egloskerry in the early 1950s. Lens Of Sutton

The view from an N class 2-6-0 as it enters the cutting approaching Launceston with an Up working in the mid-1950s. Mike Daly

On 21 October 1961 Exmouth Junction's N class 2-6-0 31844 brings an Up passenger train out of the cutting towards Launceston. Terry Nicholls

Launceston SR station and yard in the 1920s. The GWR station and Goods shed is immediately behind the SR building.
Reginald T. Reeves/Exmoor Heritage Postcards

The LSWR station at Launceston around 1920 with the GWR station on the right. Part of the joint double signal box is visible in the centre of the photo.

The Up platform at Launceston SR station from which a train is departing past the double signal box in the mid-1940s. A train hauled by a Laira 4575 class 2-6-2T has arrived at the GWR station.

The SR side of the double signal box at Launceston in the early 1950s with the GWR station in the background.
Lens Of Sutton

In 1958 Exmouth Junction's Battle Of Britain class 4-6-2 34061 '73 Squadron' enters Launceston on a service to Exeter Central. Laira's 4575 class 2-6-2T 4592 has arrived on a train from Plymouth and has uncoupled. It is taking water before running round. Norman Simmons/Hugh Davies Photos

In the mid-1920s Exmouth Junction's N class 2-6-0 833 is at Launceston on a train to Padstow as an Up train departs.

On 27 April 1963 restored T9 class 4-4-0 120 is at Launceston with Plymouth Railway Circle's 'North Cornishman' Railtour on the way to Wadebridge. The train was formed from BR Standard Set 519. Maurice Dart

In the mid-1950s Exmouth Junction's T9 class 4-4-0 30709 is at Launceston on a service to Exeter Central. The GWR loco shed is in the centre of the photo. David Lawrence/Hugh Davies Photos

The small SR loco shed at Launceston in June 1954. Laira's 4575 class 2-6-2T 5569 waits to depart with a train to Plymouth North Road. Rail Archive Stephenson (Photomatic)

Laira's 4575 class 2-6-2T 5531 has run through the SR Launceston loco shed and has turned ready for the return trip to Plymouth North Road on 25 June 1955. Maurice Dart/Transport Treasury

In Spring 1962 Laira's 4575 class 2-6-2T 5544 has arrived at Launceston SR on a train from Plymouth.
R. K. Blencowe Collection

On 25 September 1961 Laira's 8750 class 0-6-0PT 4656 passes the decrepit SR loco shed at Launceston. Freight stock occupies the GWR yard.

In 1959 Laira's 8750 class 0-6-0PT 9711 stands near the SR loco shed.

In the mid-1950s Laira's 8750 class 0-6-0PT 9770 waits to depart from Launceston SR with a train to Plymouth North Road. The train is composed of London Midland Region stock. Real Photographs Co. Ltd.

9
THE GREAT WESTERN SOCIETY AT BODMIN

From 1969 until October 1977 this Society operated a small site at Bodmin General centred on the GWR loco shed.

1361 class 0-6-0ST 1363 pulls away from Bodmin Road for Bodmin General with two GWR non-corridor coaches on 1 May 1969. This loco moved to the Great Western Society at Didcot.

1363 and 0-4-0ST 'Devonport Dockyard No. 19' (WB 2962/1950) outside the loco shed at Bodmin General on 11 April 1974. This loco is based at Bodmin but has spent a period on loan to the Pontypool & Blaenavon Railway. C. H. S. Owen

The Great Western Society at Bodmin

On 1 May 1969 1363 is attached to two GWR carriages at Bodmin General.

On 22 July 1972 1363 enters Bodmin General with Hawksworth coach 7372 on a train during an Open Day.

On 11 April 1974 1363 and Hawksworth carriage 7372 prepare to leave Bodmin General for an Open Weekend at Par Harbour hauled by St Blazey's 08 class 350hp 0-6-0 diesel shunter 08841 (ex D4009). Nick Castle

The preserved LSWR Permanent Way Trolley now named 'CAMEL' on exhibition at Bodmin General on 11 July 1970. For many years this trolley was housed in a shed at Boscarne Junction which stood on the original trackbed. The decrepit shed still exists and the trolley resides at Bodmin General. Ken Webber

10

THE BODMIN & WENFORD RAILWAY

In 1985 the Bodmin Railway Preservation Society was formed with a base at Bodmin General. Amalgamation with the Bugle-based Cornish Steam Locomotive Preservation Society followed in 1987. Renaming to The Bodmin Steam Railway followed which was later changed to the present title. Services and facilities have been steadily developed as the years progressed. The photos in this section are arranged in chronological order. Builders' details are only mentioned in the first shot of each loco where appropriate. I have attempted to show every loco which has worked on the line.

At Bodmin General awaiting restoration to commence on 4 September 1988 are Class 52 C-C 2700hp Diesel Hydraulic D1048 'WESTERN LADY' and 4575 class 2-6-2T 5552. The Hydraulic moved to the Midland Railway Centre. Maurice Dart

This old boiler at Bodmin General on 4 September 1988 was obtained from a farm near Calstock. After some months it departed to an unknown location. Behind it, outside the shed is 0-4-0D 'PROGRESS' (JF 4000001/1945) which can now be seen at the Tarka Railway Group at Torrington. Maurice Dart

On a very inclement 28 October 1989 the first services were operated to Bodmin Parkway but were not 'platformed' there. The workings were 'top & tailed' and 08444 headed the train into Bodmin General. Maurice Dart

At Bodmin General bringing up the rear of the return working from Bodmin Parkway on 28 October 1989 is 0-4-0ST 'DEVONPORT DOCKYARD No. 19'. (WB 2962/1950) Maurice Dart

A line of stock on Barracks siding on 18 April 1991 includes Railbus W79976 which moved to the Colne Valley Railway, the frames and wheels of 0-4-0ST 'PROGRESS' (P 1611/1923) which moved to the Swanage Railway and 0-4-0 Fireless WB 3121/1957 which is at Bodmin awaiting restoration. Maurice Dart

Two visiting locos at Bodmin Parkway on 8 October 1991, awaiting return to their home bases, are Diesel Hydraulics 1700hp B-B Hymek D7017 and class 52 C-C D1010 'WESTERN CAMPAIGNER' which is disguised as D1035 'WESTERN YEOMAN'. Maurice Dart

On 31 May 1992 visiting City class 4-4-0 3440 'CITY OF TRURO' waits to depart from Bodmin General. In the right background visible through the haze of steam is 0-6-0ST 'GLENDOWER' (HE 3810/1954) which was on loan from the South Devon Railway for a period. Maurice Dart

Visiting City class 4-4-0 3440 'CITY OF TRURO' has arrived at Bodmin General at 17.20 on 3 June 1992. In the distance by the overline bridge is 4wDM 'CORRALL' ,(RH 242867/1946) which moved to the North Downs Steam Railway. Maurice Dart

A freight service for Fitzgerald Lighting operated for two periods. On 10 September 1992 class 08 350hp 0-6-0 Diesel shunter D3559 (08444) has arrived at Walker Lines sidings with a Cargowagon which 0-4-0D 'PROGRESS' is moving towards to shunt to a nearby line.
Maurice Dart

On the dull early evening of 22 September 1992 visiting class 20 1000hp B-B Diesel D8110 stands outside the workshop at Bodmin. In the background alongside the water tank is 0-6-0ST 'SWIFTSURE' (HE 2857/1943).
Maurice Dart

Visiting Psuedo-USA 0-6-0T 30075 failed on a late afternoon service from Bodmin Parkway on 14 September 1993. The train was rescued by diesel shunter D3559 which is propelling 30075 to the Pit road At Bodmin General. On the right is class 50 2700hp Co-Co Diesel 50042 TRIUMPH'. Maurice Dart

On 29 March 1994 visiting 5700 class 0-6-0PT 7752 stands in the depot yard at Bodmin. On the right is class 20 1000hp B-B Diesel 20166. Two boilers from locos undergoing overhaul are in the background. Maurice Dart

Visiting 5700 class 0-6-0PT 7714 stands in the depot yard at Bodmin on 13 September 1995. Maurice Dart

Two locos stabled at Walker Lines on 16 January 1996 are class 20 Diesel 20166 and 0-6-0ST 75178 (WB 2766/1944). Maurice Dart

Visiting 4500 class 2-6-2T 4561 is stopped at Colesloggett Halt on the 15.35 service from Bodmin Parkway on 10 August 1996. Maurice Dart

A 'V.I. P. Special' is at Boscarne Junction with civic dignitaries on board and B & W Railway Officials to perform the official opening ceremony of the newly constructed station at 13.00hr on 14 August 1996. The train is formed from DMUs 53980 and 52054. Maurice Dart

On 31 January 1997, to celebrate the Author's 65th birthday, a special train to Boscarne Junction was arranged. It was hauled by class 20 Diesel 20166 and the loco has run round the Toad brake van which formed the train. The loco propelled the van down the track and was 'secured' before the crew along with invited guests departed to the Borough Arms at Dunmere for a meal. This followed the time-honoured tradition unofficially carried out by crews working Wenford branch trains but of course their train stopped adjacent to Dunmere Crossing. Maurice Dart

On very wet 10 February 1997 0-6-0T 7597 (RSHN 7597/1949) which was unofficially called 'ZEBEDEE' because of its ungainly motion at certain speeds waits to depart from Bodmin Parkway after working a 'Funeral' train from Bodmin General. This loco moved to Peak Rail at Matlock. Maurice Dart/Transport Treasury

Visiting 4800 class 0-4-2T 1450 stands with the freshly-restored visiting Auto coach at Bodmin General on 4 May 1997. 0-6-0ST 'Swiftsure' is in the background. Maurice Dart

On 7 September 1997 visiting 2251 class 0-6-0 3205 waits to depart from Boscarne Junction. Maurice Dart/Transport Treasury

The Bodmin & Wenford Railway

A visitor on 21 September 1997 was Class 31 A1A-A1A 1250hp Diesel 31273 which waits to depart from Bodmin General. Maurice Dart

Under restoration in the workshop at Bodmin on 25 February 1998 is 2884 class 2-8-0 3802 which subsequently moved to the Llangollen Railway. Maurice Dart

On 16 May 1998, after a day's work, visiting King class 4-6-0 6024 'KING EDWARD I' stands on the servicing pit at Bodmin. In the background is 0-6-0ST 62 'Ugly' (RSHN 7673/1950) which moved to the Vale Of Glamorgan Railway. *Maurice Dart/ Transport Treasury*

Working the Fitzgerald Freight involved quite complex shunting at Bodmin Parkway to exchange wagons. Here, on 3 June 1998 Class 20 20166 'RIVER FOWEY' is sandwiched between two sets of Cargowagons. *Maurice Dart*

On 3 June 1998 class 37 1750hp Co-Co Diesel 37671 'TRE POL AND PEN' departs from Bodmin Parkway yard with loaded Cargowagons from Fitzgerald Lighting at Walker Lines. The class 37 took the train to Liskeard where it would run round and return the train to St Blazey yard for onward transit. Maurice Dart

After the loaded train had departed on 3 June 1998 20166 'RIVER FOWEY' waits at the platform at Bodmin Parkway to deliver empty Cargowagons to Walker Lines. Maurice Dart

On 27 August 1998 visiting 1500 class 0-6-0PT 1501 stands on the servicing pit in front of 0-6-0T 7597 at Bodmin after completing its duties. Maurice Dart

In October 1998 two locos visited the railway after working a Railtour to Penzance. On 25 October Black 5 4-6-0 45110 waits to set off from Bodmin General to run to Bodmin Parkway and onwards to work the return Railtour. In the distance 20166 is stabled by the overline bridge and class 33 Diesel 33110 is on the left. Maurice Dart

The other visitor, 8F 2-8-0 48773 waits to depart from Bodmin General on 25 October 1998. Maurice Dart

On 9 May 1999 visiting V2 class 2-6-2 60800 'GREEN ARROW' waits to depart on an afternoon service from Bodmin Parkway. Maurice Dart

Visiting 4575 class 2-6-2T 5541 runs around its train at Bodmin Parkway on 26 August 1999.

On 2 October 1999 visiting Class 66 3200hp Co-Co Diesel 66125 runs around the train at Bodmin Parkway.

Visiting class 47 2750hp Co-Co Diesel 47736 'CAMBRIDGE TRACTION & ROLLING STOCK DEPOT' rests against the buffers at Bodmin General on 2 October 1999.

On 8 June 2000 Her Majesty Queen Elizabeth II accompanied by Prince Phillip visited Bodmin and arrived on a special train over the line. Carrying the special four headlamp code denoting a 'Royal Train' it is entering Bodmin General headed by 0-6-0ST 62 'UGLY' which is piloting visiting 8750 class 0-6-0PT 9682. Stabled inside the running shed is class 10 350hp 0-6-0 Diesel shunter B3452. Maurice Dart

The Royal Train hauled by 0-6-0ST 62 'UGLY' and visiting 8750 class 0-6-0PT 9682 arrives at Bodmin General on 8 June 2000. Civic dignitaries and B & W Railway Directors and Staff wait on the platform to welcome the Royal visitors. Myself and another volunteer were granted privileged access to the end of the platform to record the occasion. Maurice Dart

On 3 September 2000 visiting 4800 class 0-4-2T 1420 pilots 0-6-0T 7597 on a service waiting to depart from Bodmin Parkway. Maurice Dart

Two visiting Diesel locos were at the railway on 7 October 2000. Standing alongside 20166 'RIVER FOWEY' at Bodmin General are class 67 3200hp Bo-Bo 67008 and class 66 3200hp Co-Co 66161. Maurice Dart

On 28 March 2001 standing in front of class 50 2700hp Co-Co Diesel 50042 'TRIUMPH' at Bodmin General is visiting class 50 D449. This loco had for a period been converted to work clay trains during which time it was renumbered to 50149. It had been named 'DEFIANCE'. Maurice Dart

Also present at Bodmin General on 28 March 2001 was Warship class 2200hp B-B Diesel Hydraulic D821 'CORNWALL'. The loco had been renamed from 'GREYHOUND' at Falmouth Docks four days earlier.
Maurice Dart

Waiting to depart from Boscarne Junction on 1 September 2001 is visiting Ivatt 2MT 2-6-2T 41312. At the rear is 0-6-0ST 62 'UGLY'. Maurice Dart

The Bodmin & Wenford Railway

Visiting ex Port Talbot Railway 0-6-0ST 813 pilots 8750 0-6-0PT 4612 on a train passing the running shed entering Bodmin General on 8 September 2002. On shed ae 0-4-0ST 'ALFRED' (WB 3058/1953) and visiting 1366 class 0-6-0PT 1369.

A train waiting to depart from Boscarne Junction on 6 September 2003 is double-headed by 4575 class 2-6-2Ts 5552 and visiting 5542. Maurice Dart

On 20 September 2003 Bodmin General was host to three visitors which were a TPO coach and two Diesel locos. The locos are class 66 3200hp Co-Co 66241 and class 67 3200hp Bo-Bo 67009. Maurice Dart

0-6-0ST 'SWIFTSURE' is running round the train at Bodmin Parkway on 17 June 2004. Maurice Dart

On 17 July 2004 Class 33 1550hp Bo-Bo Diesel 33110 stands in front of class 37 1750hp Co-Co 37142 at Bodmin General. Maurice Dart

Bettie Well 2-4-0WT 30587 departs from Bodmin Parkway on a brake van special on 17 July 2004. Maurice Dart

Stabled at Bodmin General on 7 August 2004 are 350hp 0-6-0 Diesel shunters class 10 D3452 and class 08 08444. Maurice Dart

Resting outside the Workshop at Bodmin on 7 August 2004 is 0-4-0ST 'DEVONPORT DOCKYARD No. 19. Maurice Dart

On 1 September 2004 8750 class 0-6-0PT 4612 sets off from Bodmin Parkway on the climb to Bodmin General.
Maurice Dart

Three locos stabled at Walker Lines on 4 September 2004 are 350hp 0-6-0 Deisel shunters class 10 D3452 and class 08 08444 along with 0-4-0 Diesel 'PROGRESS'. Maurice Dart

The boiler off M7 class 0-4-4T 30053 arrived at Bodmin from the Swanage Railway for overhaul and is outside the workshop on 2 March 2005. Maurice Dart

Stock used to be stored in the open in the sidings in Bodmin Parkway yard but nowadays it is under cover in a new storage shed which has been erected on the site. On 2 June 2005 0-4-0D 'PETER' (JF 22928/1940) awaits restoration in Parkway yard. Maurice Dart

Left: Alongside the rebuilt signal box at Bodmin General on permanent display is the Smokebox Wrapper Plate from Liskeard & Caradon Railway 0-6-0ST 'CARADON seen on 28 June 2005. For many years this was utilised as a toilet placed over a stream alongside Moorswater loco shed. Maurice Dart

Below: Recorded on 28 June 2005 at Bodmin General is the LSWR Permanent Way Trolley now named 'CAMEL'. This trolley was built by the LSWR in 1875 and was stabled permanently in a wooden shed in the fork of the two lines at Dunmere Junction which was on the original formation of the line to Bodmin Wharf. Maurice Dart

On 13 May 2006 4575 class 2-6-2T 5552 executes a storming 'run-past' at Colesloggett Halt for visiting members of Launceston Railway Circle. Maurice Dart

Waiting to depart from Boscarne Junction on 2 September 2006 is visiting 5101 class 2-6-2T 4160. Maurice Dart

Following restoration at Bodmin West Country class 4-6-2 34007 'WADEBRIDGE' waits to depart from Boscarne Junction on 28 October 2006 with the first passenger train it worked. This loco moved to the Mid-Hants Railway. Maurice Dart

On 28 October 2006 visiting Beattie Well 2-4-0WT 30585 pilots classmate 30587 on a demonstration Goods at Bodmin General. The fire in the brake van is obviously in use. Maurice Dart

4wDM NDS 3 'LEC' (RH 443642/1960) shunts stock at Bodmin Parkway yard on 20 February 2007. This loco has been renamed 'BRIAN' in memory of its deceased owner and long serving volunteer. Maurice Dart

On 20 February 2007 class 20 1000hp Bo-Bo Diesel 20197 stands at end of the Down siding outside Bodmin General. This loco never operated on the railway and was used as a source of spares for 20166. When on this siding it was nicknamed 'Our Permanent Buffer Stop'. Both of the class 20s departed to Harry Needle Railways. Maurice Dart

On Barracks siding on 20 February 2007 are class 20 20166, the Steam Crane, class 37 37142 and class 50 50042 'TRIUMPH'. Maurice Dart

The same line on Barracks siding on 20 February 2007 with class 37 37142 and class 50 50042 'TRIUMPH' prominent. Maurice Dart

The Bodmin & Wenford Railway

On 4 April 2007 class 47 2750hp Co-Co Diesel 47306 once called 'THE SAPPER' stands at Bodmin General. This loco was restored to traffic at Bodmin. Maurice Dart

Visiting 4575 class 2-6-2T 5553 runs round the train at Bodmin Parkway in September 2007.

Standing in front of 8750 class 0-6-0PT 4612 at Bodmin General on 22 March 2008 is visiting A1X class 'Terrier' 0-6-0T 2670 'BODIAM'. Maurice Dart

Two ColasRail owned class 47s visited the railway and on 5 April 2008 47727 'REBECCA' stands at Bodmin General. Maurice Dart

From the left at Bodmin General on 5 April 2008 are 47727 'REBECCA', 50042 'TRIUMPH', ColasRail 47749 'DEMELZA' and 47306 'THE SAPPER'. Maurice Dart

A visitor at Bodmin General on 5 September 2008 was 1366 class 0-6-0PT 1369. Maurice Dart

Following the restoration to traffic of both of the 'Par Harbour Twins' a rededication ceremony was held at Bodmin General on 8 April 2009. Both locos entered the station on parallel lines working demonstration Goods trains. Here are 0-4-0STs 'JUDY' (WB 2572/1937) and 'ALFRED' (WB 3058/1953). Maurice Dart

A very unusual visitor to the railway was 5600 class 0-6-2T 5619 which is on a train ready to depart from Boscarne Junction on 4 September 2009. This was the first visit by one of this class west of Newton Abbot where they could be seen occasionally visiting the Loco Works. Maurice Dart

More visiting locos appeared on the railway on 17 April 2010 when 4575 class 2-6-2Ts 5526 and 5521 are entering Bodmin Parkway on a service from Bodmin General. Maurice Dart

On shed at Bodmin on 1 September 2010 are T9 class 4-4-0 120 and visiting M7 class 0-4-4T 53. The base of the coal stage is the original structure. The M7 is standing over an inspection pit which was outside the original one-road loco shed. A two-road shed was built over both inspection pits. The back pit was inside the original structure. Maurice Dart

Departing from Bodmin Parkway in 2010 is 4200 class 2-8-0T 4247.

Climbing around Check Rail curve on a service from Boscarne Junction on 13 February 2011 is 6400 class 0-6-0PT 6435.
Maurice Dart

On display at Bodmin General on 23 June 2011 after failing with blocked tubes is visiting A1X class 'Terrier' 0-6-0T 32662 which was once named 'MARTELLO'. Maurice Dart

Visiting O2 class 0-4-4T W24 'CALBOURNE' from the Isle Of Wight Railway coupled to resident T9 class 'Greyhound' 4-4-0 30120 back on to a train at Bodmin Parkway on 22 April 2012. Maurice Dart

The latest visitor to our railway at the time this book was compiled was Standard 4MT 2-6-4T 80104 which is running around at Bodmin Parkway on 26 May 2012. This was during a special weekend to celebrate the 125th anniversary of the opening of the line from Bodmin Road to Bodmin.

11
THE LAUNCESTON STEAM RAILWAY

This 600mm gauge line laid on the SR trackbed opened on 28 December 1983 and has steadily developed over the years. It has been visited by several guest locos. I have attempted to show most of the locos. The photos are arranged in chronological order.

On 27 July 2003 0-4-0ST 'LILIAN' (HE 317/1883) waits to depart from the outer terminus of the line at New Mills. Maurice Dart/Transport Treasury

0-4-0ST 'LILIAN' is stopped at Canna Park on a train to Launceston on 27 July 2003.
Maurice Dart

On 27 July 2003 0-4-0ST 'LILIAN' approaches Hunts Crossing on the way to Launceston. Maurice Dart

0-4-0ST 'VELINHELI' (HE 409/1886) receives some attention before departing from Launceston on 8 July 2004. Maurice Dart

In the upper yard at Launceston on 8 July 2004 is 0-4-0ST 'COVERTCOAT' (HE 679/1898). Maurice Dart

This home-made 4wBE in the Stock shed at Launceston on 8 July 2004 was formerly a 2w + 2wBE.
Maurice Dart

Ready to depart for shipment to Alabama a few days later 0-4-2ST 'DAME ANN' sits in the Stock shed at Launceston on 8 July 2004. This loco which was built by the Exmoor Steam Railway had run trials at Launceston.
Maurice Dart

A locomotive from London's Post Office Tube Railway is stored beneath the overline bridge at Launceston on 8 May 2005. Maurice Dart

On 8 May 2005 4wDM No.2 (MR 5646/1933) is inside the gas works shed at Launceston. Maurice Dart

Also in the gas works shed at Launceston on 8 May 2005 was 4wDM No. 3 which may be FH 1896/1935. Maurice Dart

On 7 July 2009 home built 0-4-0VBT 89 is in the stock shed at Launceston. Maurice Dart

Also in the stock shed at Launceston on 7 July 2009 was this home made 4wPE which was formerly a 2-2w PE. Maurice Dart

During an Indian Hill Railway weekend held at the railway Darjeeling and Himalayan Railway 0-4-2ST 19 enters Launceston on 19 August 2009. Maurice Dart

The Launceston Steam Railway

Suitably decorated for the Indian railway weekend 0-4-0ST 'LILIAN' driven by Nigel Bowman enters Launceston on 19 August 2009. Maurice Dart

Visiting 0-6-0T 'GERTRUDE' (AB1578/1918) runs round the train at New Mills on 30 October 2009. Maurice Dart

In the gas works shed at Launceston on 20 September 2010 was this home-built 4-4w battery railcar. Maurice Dart

In grey undercoat fresh after being completely overhauled by Kay Bowman 0-4-0ST 'DOROTHEA (HE 763/1901) is inside the gas works shed at Launceston on 20 September 2010. Maurice Dart

Built by the Ffestiniog Railway at Boston Lodge Works, visiting 2-6-2T 'LYD' was in the upper yard at Launceston on 20 September 2010. Maurice Dart

On 27 October 2010 visiting 4wVBT Roanoke (0507/2003) shunts wagons at Launceston, driven by its owner, John Spenceley. Maurice Dart

LOCATION INDEX

Barracks Siding and Bodmin Down Siding 113, 140

Bodmin GWR/General 19-31, 108-112, 114-117, 120-122, 124, 125, 127-134, 136, 139, 141-145, 147

Bodmin Road/Parkway 10-18, 108, 113, 119, 122, 123, 125, 126, 128,132, 133, 135, 136, 139, 141, 145-148

Bodmin SR/North 36, 37, 39-42

Bodmin Town Wharf 37, 38

Boscarne Junction 32, 43, 52-54, 118-120, 130, 131, 138, 144

Camelford 95

Canna Park 150

Check Rail Curve 146

Colesloggett Halt 118, 137

Delabole 93

Delabole Quarry 94

De Lank Incline 51

Dunmere Crossings 33, 34

Dunmere Halt 34, 35

Dunmere Junction 32, 33, 43

Egloskerry 98

Grogley 55-57

Guineaport 60

Hunts Crossing 150

Launceston LSR 151-159

Launceston SR 98-107

Kittle Petherick 83

Nanstallon 55

New Mills 149, 157

Otterham 96

Padstow 83-89

Penhargard 44

Port Isaac Road 92

Ruthern Bridge 57, 58

St Kew Highway 90, 91

Stump Oak 45

Trelill Tunnel 92

Tresarrett 44

Tresmeer 97

Wadebridge Junction 58, 59, 90

Wadebridge Quay 81

Wadebridge Shed 62-67, 69-73, 76, 79

Wadebridge Station, east and west 61, 63-66, 68-71, 73-82

Walker Lines 115, 117, 135

Wenford 45-47

Wenford Bridge 47-50